A POCKETFUL OF
PYTHON

PICKED
BY
TERRY
GILLIAM

WITH A PREFACE BY ERIC IDLE

methuen

WRITTEN AND CONCEIVED BY
GRAHAM CHAPMAN, JOHN CLEESE TERRY GILLIAM, ERIC IDLE TERRY JONES AND MICHAEL PALIN

DESIGN BY KATY HEPBURN AND ALUN EVANS

Co-ordinating editor for the *Pocketful of Python* series: Geoffrey Strachan
The texts included in this volume are taken from the TV scripts for *Monty Python's Flying Circus*, published by Methuen in 1989 as *Monty Python's Flying Circus: Just the Words*; the film screenplays for *Monty Python and the Holy Grail*, *The Life of Brian* (with *Montypythonscrapbook*) and *The Meaning of Life*, published by Methuen in 1977, 1979, and 1983; *Monty Python's Big Red Book* (Methuen 1971); *The Brand New Monty Python Bok*, published in paperback as *The Brand New Monty Python Papperbok* (Methuen 1973 and 1974); and *The Fairly Incomplete and Rather Badly Illustrated Monty Python Song Book* (1994)

Published by Methuen 2000
1 3 5 7 9 10 8 6 4 2
First published in Great Britain by
Methuen Publishing Limited 215 Vauxhall Bridge Road, London SW1V 1EJ

in the same series

A Pocketful of Python picked by Terry Jones
A Pocketful of Python picked by John Cleese
A Pocketful of Python picked by Michael Palin

Methuen Publishing Limited Reg. No 3543167
A CIP catalogue record for this title is available from the British Library

ISBN 0 413 75010 8
Printed and bound in Singapore by Tien Wah Press

INTRODUCTION

Dear reader, or browser (if you happen to be one of those cheap bastards that hang about in bookstores fingering the goods, foxing the pages, scuffing the dust jackets with no intention of ever shelling out) here is your chance to take part in the greatest historical event of our age – SAVING THE COMEDY RAINFORESTS.

As you know, they are being RAVAGED at an ever increasing rate by GREEDY COMEDIANS who have no interest in the sustainable maintenance of these riches – interested only in the QUICK GAG, the SNAPPY ONE-LINER, the SMART-ARSE PUNCH LINE. Do they ever consider how long it takes for a good joke to mature? No! Their only concern is their own immediate gratification, satisfying the TV audience's insatiable demand for NEW LAUGHS!

Well, here is your chance to help.

All the material in this book is GUARANTEED TO BE OLD! RECYCLED! Old, recycled comic material from the legendary Monty Python team. NOTHING NEW! Not a single new joke or idea has been sacrificed for this tome.

By buying this book you are helping to preserve a FUNNY, LAUGH-FILLED FUTURE for your children – assuming they don't die when global warming melts the icecaps and causes the seas to rise and drown Norfolk and other low-lying areas of Britain including that bit of land where Sizewell B is located, causing unparalleled leakages of deadly radioactive material which will wipe out all the sea life around this island forever, or maybe, even, cause A NUCLEAR DISASTER THAT WILL MAKE CHERNOBYL LOOK LIKE A TEDDY BEAR'S PICNIC!!!!.

OK, buying this book is, in the long term, absolutely pointless. But, if you are one of those cheap bastards browsing your way through these pages, count yourself lucky – this hasn't cost you a penny.

If, however, you've already paid for the book, see page 59.

T.G. February 2000

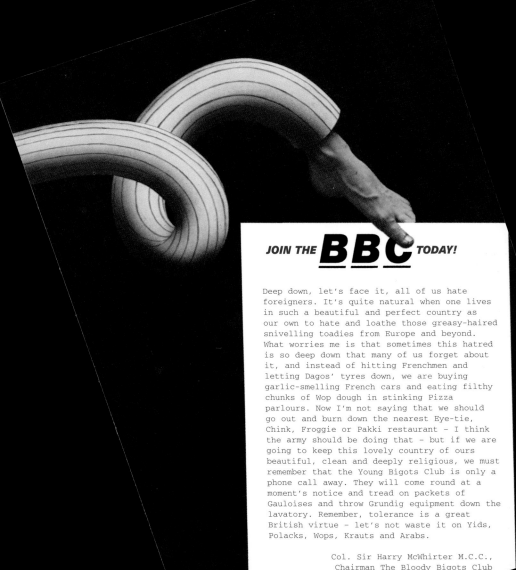

JOIN THE **BBC** TODAY!

Deep down, let's face it, all of us hate foreigners. It's quite natural when one lives in such a beautiful and perfect country as our own to hate and loathe those greasy-haired snivelling toadies from Europe and beyond. What worries me is that sometimes this hatred is so deep down that many of us forget about it, and instead of hitting Frenchmen and letting Dagos' tyres down, we are buying garlic-smelling French cars and eating filthy chunks of Wop dough in stinking Pizza parlours. Now I'm not saying that we should go out and burn down the nearest Eye-tie, Chink, Froggie or Pakki restaurant - I think the army should be doing that - but if we are going to keep this lovely country of ours beautiful, clean and deeply religious, we must remember that the Young Bigots Club is only a phone call away. They will come round at a moment's notice and tread on packets of Gauloises and throw Grundig equipment down the lavatory. Remember, tolerance is a great British virtue - let's not waste it on Yids, Polacks, Wops, Krauts and Arabs.

Col. Sir Harry McWhirter M.C.C.,
Chairman The Bloody Bigots Club

THE MEANING OF LIFE

Why are we here, what is life all about?
Is God really real, or is there some doubt?
Well tonight we're going to sort it all out,
For tonight it's the Meaning of Life.

What's the point of all these hoax?
Is it the chicken and egg time, are we just yolks?
Or perhaps we're just one of God's little jokes,
Well *ça c'est* the Meaning of Life.

Is life just a game where we make up the rules
While we're searching for something to say
Or are we just simply spiralling coils
Of self-replicating DNA?

What is life? What is our fate?
Is there Heaven and Hell? Do we reincarnate?
Is mankind evolving or is it too late?
Well tonight here's the Meaning of Life.

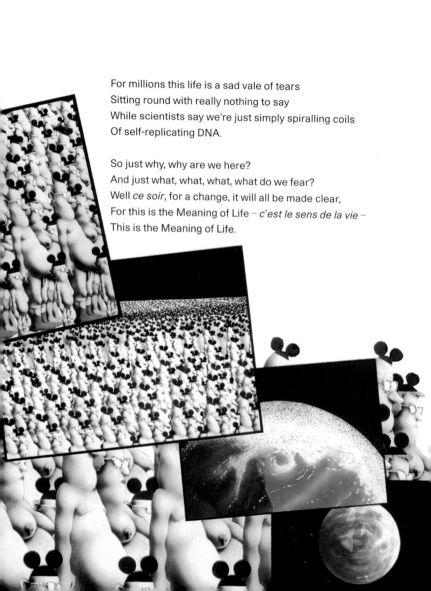

For millions this life is a sad vale of tears
Sitting round with really nothing to say
While scientists say we're just simply spiralling coils
Of self-replicating DNA.

So just why, why are we here?
And just what, what, what, what do we fear?
Well *ce soir*, for a change, it will all be made clear,
For this is the Meaning of Life – *c'est le sens de la vie* –
This is the Meaning of Life.

DAMMIT!
DAMMIT!!
DAMMIT!!

CAREERS ADVICE FOR
MR ANCHOVY

MR ANCHOVY *is standing waiting beside a* COUNSELLOR *sitting at a desk.*

COUNSELLOR: Ah Mr Anchovy. Do sit down.

ANCHOVY: Thank you. Take the weight off the feet, eh?

COUNSELLOR: Yes, yes.

ANCHOVY: Lovely weather for the time of year, I must say.

COUNSELLOR: Enough of this gay banter. And now Mr Anchovy, you asked us to advise you which job in life you were best suited for.

ANCHOVY: That is correct, yes.

COUNSELLOR: Well I now have the results here of the interviews and the aptitude tests that you took last week, and from them we've built up a pretty clear picture of the sort of person that you are. And I think I can say, without fear of contradiction, that the ideal job for you is chartered accountancy.

ANCHOVY: But I *am* a chartered accountant.

COUNSELLOR: Jolly good. Well back to the office with you then.

ANCHOVY: No! No! No! You don't understand. I've been a chartered

accountant for the last twenty years. I want a new job. Something *exciting* that will let me *live*.

COUNSELLOR: Well chartered accountancy is rather exciting isn't it?

ANCHOVY: Exciting? No it's *not*. It's dull. Dull. *Dull*. My God it's dull, it's so desperately dull and tedious and stuffy and boring and des-per-ate-ly DULL.

COUNSELLOR: Well, er, yes Mr Anchovy, but you see your report here says that you are an extremely dull person. You see, our experts describe you as an appallingly dull fellow, unimaginative, timid, lacking in initiative, spineless, easily dominated, no sense of humour, tedious company and irrepressibly drab and awful. And whereas in most professions these would be considerable drawbacks, in chartered accountancy they are a positive boon.

ANCHOVY: But don't you see, I came here to find a new job, a new life, a new *meaning* to my existence. Can't you help me?

COUNSELLOR: Well, do you have any idea of what you want to do?

ANCHOVY: Yes, yes I have.

COUNSELLOR: What?

ANCHOVY *(boldly)*: Lion taming.

COUNSELLOR: Well yes. Yes. Of course, it's a bit of a jump isn't it? I mean, er, chartered accountancy to lion taming in one go. You don't think it might be better if you worked your way *towards* lion taming, say, via banking . . .

ANCHOVY: No, no, no, no. No. I don't want to wait. At nine o'clock tomorrow I want to be in there, taming.

COUNSELLOR: Fine, fine. But do you, do you have any qualifications?

ANCHOVY: Yes, I've got a hat.

COUNSELLOR: A hat?

ANCHOVY: Yes, a hat. A lion taming hat. A hat with 'lion tamer' on it. I got it at Harrods. And it lights up saying 'lion tamer' in great big neon letters, so that you can tame them after dark when they're less stroppy.

COUNSELLOR: I see, I see.

ANCHOVY: And you can switch it off during the day time, and claim reasonable wear and tear as allowable professional expenses under paragraph 335C . . .

COUNSELLOR: Yes, yes, yes, I do follow, Mr Anchovy, but you see the snag is . . . if I now call Mr Chipperfield and say to him, 'look here, I've got a forty-five-year-old chartered accountant with me who wants to become a lion tamer', his first question is not going to be 'does he have his own hat?' He's going to ask what sort of experience you've had with lions.

ANCHOVY: Well I . . . I've seen them at the zoo.

COUNSELLOR: Good, good, good.

ANCHOVY: Little brown furry things with short stumpy legs and great long noses. I don't know what all the fuss is about, I could tame one of those. They look pretty tame to start with.

COUNSELLOR: And these, er, these lions . . . how high are they?

ANCHOVY (indicating a height of one foot): Well they're about so high, you know. They don't frighten me at all.

COUNSELLOR: Really. And do these lions eat ants?

ANCHOVY: Yes, that's right.

COUNSELLOR: Er, well, Mr Anchovy . . . I'm afraid what you've got hold of there is an anteater.

ANCHOVY: A what?

COUNSELLOR: An anteater. Not a lion. You see a lion is a huge savage beast, about five feet high, ten feet long, weighing about four

hundred pounds, running at forty miles per hour, with masses of sharp pointed teeth and nasty long razor-sharp claws that can rip your belly open before you can say 'Eric Robinson', and they look like this.

The counsellor produces large picture of a lion and shows it to Mr Anchovy who screams and passes out. He then sits up with a start.

COUNSELLOR: Now, shall I call Mr Chipperfield?

ANCHOVY: Er, no, no, no. I think your idea of making the transition to lion taming via easy stages, say via insurance . . .

COUNSELLOR: Or banking.

ANCHOVY: Or banking, yes, yes, banking that's a man's life, isn't it? Banking, travel, excitement, adventure, thrills, decisions affecting people's lives.

COUNSELLOR: Jolly good, well, er, shall I put you in touch with a bank?

ANCHOVY: Yes.

COUNSELLOR: Fine.

ANCHOVY: Er . . . no, no, no. Look, er, it's a big decision, I'd like a couple of weeks to think about it . . . er . . . you know, don't want to jump into it too quickly. Maybe three weeks. I could let you know definitely then, I just don't want to make this definite decision. I'm, er . . . *(He continues muttering nervously to himself)*

COUNSELLOR: Well this is just one of the all too many cases on our books of chartered accountancy. The only way that we can fight this terrible debilitating social disease, is by informing the general public of its consequences, by showing young people that it's just not worth it. So, so please . . . give generously . . . to this address: The League for Fighting Chartered Accountancy, 55 Lincoln House, Basil Street, London, SW3.

BRIAN IN
GAOL

BRIAN *wakes up with a smile on his face to find himself being dragged along a cell corridor by* TWO GUARDS. *The horrible figure of the* JAILER *spits at him and flings him into a dark damp cell, slamming the iron grate behind him and turning the key hollowly in the lock.* BRIAN *slumps to the floor. A voice comes out of the darkness behind him.*

BEN: You *lucky* bastard!

BRIAN *spins round and peers into the gloom.*

BRIAN: Who's that?

In the darkness BRIAN *just makes out an emaciated figure, suspended on the wall, with his feet off the ground, by chains round his wrists. This is* BEN.

BEN: You lucky, lucky bastard.

BRIAN: What?

BEN *(with great bitterness)*: Proper little gaoler's pet, aren't we?

BRIAN *(ruffled)*: What do you mean?

21

BEN: You must have slipped him a few shekels, eh!

BRIAN: Slipped him a few shekels! You saw him spit in my face!

BEN: Ohhh! What wouldn't I give to be spat at in the face! I sometimes hang awake at nights dreaming of being spat at in the face.

BRIAN: Well, it's not exactly friendly, is it? They had me in manacles.

BEN: Manacles! Oooh. *(His eyes go quite dreamy)* My idea of heaven is to be allowed to be put in manacles . . . just for a few hours. They must think the sun shines out of your arse, sonny!

BRIAN: Listen! They beat me up before they threw me in here.

BEN: Oh yeah? The only day they don't beat me up is on my birthday.

BRIAN: Oh shut up.

BEN: Well, your type makes me sick! You come in here, you get treated like Royalty, and everyone outside thinks you're a bloody martyr.

BRIAN: Oh, lay off me . . . I've had a hard time!

BEN: *You've* had a hard time! Listen, sonny! I've been here five years and they only hung me the right way up yesterday!

BRIAN: All right! All right!

BEN: I just wish I had half your luck. They must think you're Lord God Almighty!

BRIAN: What'll they do to me?

BEN: Oh, you'll probably get away with crucifixion.

BRIAN: Crucifixion!

BEN: Yeah, first offence.

BRIAN: Get away with crucifixion!

BEN: Best thing the Romans ever did for us.

BRIAN *(incredulous)*: What?

BEN: Oh yeah. If we didn't have crucifixion this country would be in a right bloody mess I tell you.

BRIAN *(who can stand it no longer)*: Guard!

BEN: Nail 'em up I say!

BRIAN *(dragging himself over to the door)*: Guard!

BEN: Nail some sense into them!

GUARD *(looking through the bars)*: What do you want?

BRIAN: I want to be moved to another cell.

The GUARD *spits in his face.*

BRIAN: Oh! *(he recoils in helpless disgust)*

BEN: Oh . . . look at that! Bloody favouritism!

GUARD: Shut up, you!

BEN: Sorry! Sorry! *(He lowers his voice)* Now take my case. I've been here five years, and every night they take me down for ten minutes, then they hang me up again . . . which I regard as very fair . . . in view of what I done and if nothing else, it's taught me to respect the Romans, it's taught me that you'll never get anywhere in life unless you're prepared to do a fair day's work for a fair day's pay.

BRIAN: Oh . . . Shut up!

At that moment a CENTURION *and* TWO GUARDS *enter.*

CENTURION: Pilate wants to see you.

BRIAN: Me?

CENTURION: Come on.

BRIAN *struggles to his feet.*

BRIAN: Pilate? What does he want to see me for?

CENTURION: I think he wants to know which way up you want to be crucified.

He laughs. The TWO SOLDIERS *smirk.* BEN *laughs uproariously.*

BEN: . . . Nice one, centurion. Like it, like it.

WHAT TO DO ON MEETING
The Royal Family

This depends largely on where you meet the Royal Family. If you meet the Royal Family in a surgical supply shop, it is best not to acknowledge them *at all*, as this will only lead to embarrassment on your part, and on the part of the Royal person or persons.* However, should you meet a member of the Royal Family in normal circumstances the etiquette is clear and simple. If you are wearing a hat or turban, remove it instantly, and hold it in your *left* hand, leaving your right hand free should the Royal Personage decide on manual contact. Going down on one knee would be very much appreciated, but in a crowded supermarket or shopping precinct this could cause a great deal of congestion and end up with you getting kicked over.

NEVER touch the Royal Family under any circumstances, unless you yourself have been touched by them – and even then keep your hands well above the waist.

The correct way to address the Royal Family is 'Your Majesty' or 'Your Highness', and not 'Hello Graham'.

NEVER ask the Royal Family a direct question. For instance, should you wish to ask Princess Marina where the swimming baths are, you must say: 'The swimming baths are near here', and hope that she will say: 'No, I think you're wrong, they're over half a mile away down Thorpe Road and turn right at Hepworth's' or: 'Yes, they are near here. There they are.'

NEVER shout abuse or push or jostle the Royal Family, unless they attack *you*.

*The same applies in garages, betting shops, cinema clubs and public toilets.

GLORIA PULES & LUIGI VERCOTTI REMEMBER
THE PIRANHA BROTHERS

PULES: I walked out with Dinsdale Piranha on many occasions, and found him a charming and erudite companion. He was wont to introduce one to eminent celebrities, celebrated American singers, members of the aristocracy and other gang leaders, who he had met through his work for charities. He took a warm interest in Boys' Clubs, Sailors' Homes, Choristers' Associations and the Grenadier Guards. Mind you, there was nothing unusual about him. I should say not. Except, that Dinsdale was convinced that he was being watched by a giant hedgehog whom he referred to as 'Spiny Norman'. Normally Spiny Norman was wont to be about twelve feet from snout to tail, but when Dinsdale was depressed Norman could be anything up to eight hundred yards long. When Norman was about Dinsdale would go very quiet and start wobbling and his nose would swell up and his teeth would move about and he'd get very violent and claim that he'd laid Stanley Baldwin.

INTERVIEWER: Did it worry you that he, for example, stitched people's legs together?

PULES: Well it's better than bottling it up isn't it. He was a gentleman, Dinsdale, and what's more he knew how to treat a female impersonator.

INTERVIEWER: Most of the strange tales concern Dinsdale but what of Doug? One man who met him was Luigi Vercotti.

VERCOTTI: I had been running a successful escort agency – high class, no really, high class girls . . . we didn't have any of *that* – that was right out. So I decided to open a high class night club for the gentry at Biggleswade with International cuisine and cooking and top line acts, and not a cheap clip joint for picking up tarts . . . that was right out, I deny that completely, and one evening in walks Dinsdale with a couple of big lads, one of whom was carrying a tactical nuclear missile. They said I had bought one of their fruit machines and would I pay for it? They wanted three quarters of a million pounds.

I thought about it and I decided not to go to the Police as I had noticed that the lad with the thermonuclear device was the chief constable for the area. So a week later they called again and told me the cheque had bounced and said . . . I had to see . . . Doug.

Well, I was terrified. Everyone was terrified of Doug. I've seen grown men pull their own heads off rather than see Doug. Even Dinsdale was frightened of Doug. He used . . . sarcasm. He knew all the tricks, dramatic irony, metaphor, bathos, puns, parody, litotes and . . . satire. He was vicious.

INTERVIEWER: In this way, by a combination of violence and sarcasm, the Piranha brothers by February 1966 controlled London and the South East of England. It was in February, though, that Dinsdale made a big mistake. Latterly Dinsdale had become increasingly worried about Spiny Norman. He had come to the conclusion that Norman slept in an aeroplane hangar at Luton Airport. And so on Feb 22nd 1966, Dinsdale blew up Luton.

Well, hello and welcome to page twenty nine. In many books, page 29 is a sad anti-climax after the exciting events described on pages 27 and 28. We hope to avoid this pitfall by making our page 29 into one of the most exciting and action-packed page 29s that you've ever read. In a lot of books, page 29 contains purely descriptive matter, and in others it is still only part of the introduction, but not so this one. . . . We say: get a move on, novelists! and let's have more page 29s like this one.

of her dress as it rode up over her thighs, her slender body thrust forward by the enormous power of the 6,000 h.p. engines, as Horst hurled the car into a shrieking, sickening slide across the wet tarmac. The lion tore savagely at his bronzed thighs as the car soared into the air, turned, twisted, and plunged down the treacherous ski slope, that no man had ever survived. Tenderly Eunice caressed him as the fighters screeched out of the darkness, flames ripping towards him. The sea was coming nearer and nearer, and though neither had eaten for eight weeks, the stark terror of what they saw, gave them the last drop of energy to push their bodies to the limits. Eunice groaned, the dark figure of Shahn-el-Shid, dagger raised, hurled himself from the sheer wall of the palace. Horst reversed, swerved, coughed and threw himself into the gorge. Never had Horst known such exquisite pleasure, as far above him a million Dervishes swept into the fort, looting and pillaging. The Colonel screamed an order, and with one enormous blast the refinery was a sheet of flame – a wall of fire six miles long and eight miles high. Eunice groaned as the spacecraft roared low over the silent, darkened surface of this eerie world, a million light years from the Earth they had left only seconds before, a planet doomed to extinction, when suddenly

29

How about that for a page 29 ? Wake up Dickens! Wake up Graham Greene! Let's show the world that British literature gets on with it!

THE GERMAN
LUMBERJACK SONG

Ich bin ein Holzfäller und fühl mich stark
Ich schlaf des Nachts und hack am Tag.

CHORUS: Er ist ein Holzfäller und fühlt sich stark
Er schläft des Nachts und hackt am Tag.

Ich fälle Bäume, ich ess mein Brot
Ich geh auf das WC.
Am Mittwoch geh ich shopping
Kau Kekse zum Kaffee.

CHORUS: Er fällt die Bäume, er isst sein Brot
Er geht auf das WC.
Am Mittwoch geht er shopping
Kaut Kekse zum Kaffee.
Er ist ein Holzfäller und fühlt sich stark
Er schläft des Nachts und hackt am Tag.

Ich fälle Bäume und hupf und spring
Steck Blumen in die Vas.
Ich schlupf in Frauenkleider
Und lummel mich in Bars.

CHORUS: Er fällt Bäume, er hupft und springt
Steckt Blumen in die Vas.
Er schlupft in Frauenkleider

Und lummelt sich in Bars . . .?
Er ist ein Holzfäller und fühlt sich stark
Er schläft des Nachts und hackt am Tag.

Ich fälle Bäume, trag Stockelschuh
Und Strumpf und Bustenhalter
Wär gern ein kleines Mädchen
So wie mein Onkel Walter.

CHORUS: Er fällt die Bäume, trägt Stockelschuh
Und Strumpf und Bustenhalter . . .?

WOODY WORDS &
TINNY WORDS

An upper-class drawing room. Father, mother and daughter having tea. Four motionless servants stand behind them.

FATHER: I say . . .

DAUGHTER: Yes, Daddy?

FATHER: Croquet hoops look damn pretty this afternoon.

DAUGHTER: Frightfully damn pretty.

MOTHER: They're coming along awfully well this year.

FATHER: Yes, better than your Aunt Lavinia's croquet hoops.

DAUGHTER: Ugh! – dreadful tin things.

MOTHER: I did tell her to stick to wood.

FATHER: Yes, you can't beat wood . . . Gorn!

MOTHER: What's gorn, dear?

FATHER: Nothing, nothing, I just like the word. It gives me confidence.

Gorn . . . gorn. It's got a sort of woody quality about it. Gorn. Gorn.
Much better than 'newspaper' or 'litterbin'.

DAUGHTER: Frightful words.

MOTHER: Perfectly dreadful.

FATHER: Ugh! Newspaper! . . . litterbin . . . dreadful tinny sort of words.
Tin, tin, tin.

The daughter bursts into tears.

MOTHER: Oh, dear, don't say 'tin' to Rebecca, you know how it upsets
her.

FATHER *(to the daughter)*: Sorry old horse.

MOTHER: Sausage!

FATHER: Sausage . . . there's a good woody sort of word, 'sausage' . . .
gorn.

DAUGHTER: Antelope.

FATHER: Where? On the lawn? *(He picks up a rifle)*

DAUGHTER: No, no, daddy . . . just the word.

FATHER: Don't want an antelope nibbling the hoops.

DAUGHTER: No, antelope . . . sort of nice and woody type of thing.

MOTHER: Don't think so, Becky old chap.

FATHER: No, no 'antelope', 'antelope' – tinny sort of word *(The daughter
bursts into tears)* Oh! Sorry old man . . .

MOTHER: Really, Mansfield.

FATHER: Well, she's got to come to terms with these things . . . seemly .
. . prodding . . . vacuum . . . leap . . .

DAUGHTER *(miserably)*: Hate 'leap'.

MOTHER: Perfectly dreadful.

DAUGHTER: Sort of PVC-y sort of word, don't you know.

MOTHER: Lower-middle.

FATHER: Bound!

MOTHER: Now you're talking.

FATHER: Bound . . . Vole . . . Recidivist.

MOTHER: Bit tinny. *(The daughter howls)* Oh! Sorry, Becky old beast. *(The daughter runs out crying)*

FATHER: Oh dear, suppose she'll be gorn for a few days now.

MOTHER: Caribou!

FATHER: Splendid word.

MOTHER: No dear . . . nibbling the hoops.

FATHER *(he fires a shot)*: Caribou gorn.

MOTHER *(laughs politely)*

FATHER: Intercourse.

MOTHER: Later, dear.

FATHER: No, no, the word, 'intercourse' – good and woody . . . inter . . . course . . . pert . . . pert thighs . . . botty, botty, botty . . . *(The mother leaves the room)* . . . erogenous . . . zone . . . concubine . . . erogenous zone! Loose woman . . . erogenous zone . . .

(The mother returns and throws a bucket of water over him) Oh thank you, dear . . . you know, it's a funny thing, dear . . . all the naughty words sound woody.

MOTHER: Really, dear? . . . How about tit?

FATHER: Oh dear, I hadn't thought about that. Tit. Tit. Oh, that's very tinny isn't it? *(The daughter returns)* Ugh! Tinny, tinny . . . *(The daughter runs out crying)* Oh dear . . . ocelot . . . wasp . . . yowling . . . Oh dear, I'm bored . . . I'd better go and have a bath, I suppose.

MOTHER: Oh really, must you dear? You've had nine today.

FATHER: All right, I'll sack one of the servants . . . Simkins! . . . nasty tinny sort of name. Simkins! *(He exits)*

A pilot from the RAF banter scene* enters.

PILOT: I say, mater, cabbage crates coming over the briny.

MOTHER *(frowns and shakes her head)*: Sorry dear, don't understand.

PILOT: Er . . . cowcatchers creeping up on the conning towers . . .

MOTHER: No . . . sorry . . . old sport.

PILOT: Caribou nibbling at the croquet hoops.

---

* *See* 'A Pocketful of Python Picked by Terry Jones'.

MOTHER: Yes, Mansfield shot one in the antlers.

PILOT: Oh, jolly good show. Is 'Becca about?

MOTHER: No, she's gorn orff.

PILOT: What a super woody sort of phrase. 'Gorn orff'.

MOTHER: Yes, she's gorn orff because Mansfield said 'tin' to her.

PILOT: Oh, what rotten luck . . . oh well . . . whole afternoon to kill . . . better have a bath I suppose.

MOTHER: Oh, Gervaise do sing me a song . . .

PILOT: Oh, OK.

MOTHER: Something woody.

The pilot launches into a quite enormously loud rendering of 'She's going to marry Yum Yum'. The impact of this on the MOTHER *causes her to have a heart attack. She dies and the song ends.*

PILOT: For . . . she's going to marry Yum Yum . . . oh crikey. The old song finished her orff.

FATHER *(entering)*: What's urp?

PILOT: I'm afraid Mrs Vermin Jones appears to have passed orn.

FATHER: Dead, is she?

PILOT: 'Fraid so.

FATHER: What a blow for her.

38

THE
STORYTELLER

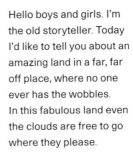

Hello boys and girls. I'm
the old storyteller. Today
I'd like to tell you about an
amazing land in a far, far
off place, where no one
ever has the wobbles.
In this fabulous land even
the clouds are free to go
where they please.

On Sundays they can go in small, well-chaperoned groups to the vast plasterboard cities that pierce the sun.

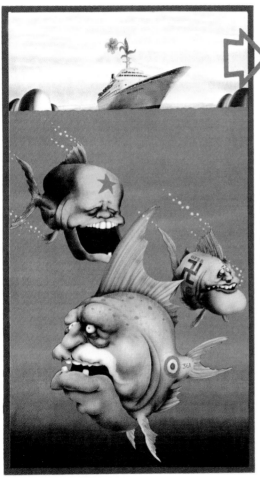

Near these cities grow shining black mountains. And near these mountains live bulging purple seas full of fishes of every known race, creed, and/or colour.

High above the water stand strange birds whose feet never quite reach the ground.

And on their wings live small brown roundish things that have amazed and astounded the crowned heads of Europe for over 300 years.

a crowned head   amazed   astounded

The birds are not the only things that don't touch the ground in this strange land. Unfortunately the topsoil is very light, too light in fact to stay in contact with the ground and so it floats 3 feet above it.

This would not be so bad, but for the fact that the people of this land do everything by fours, including walking on them.

And so, most of the people choose to live in the vast plasterboard cities where topsoil is not allowed - except a bit on Thursdays and on another day they don't have a name for. As I said, I would like to tell you about this amazing land, but the bastards who put this book together have only given me six pages and insist I finish so they can get on with the pretentious so-called funny stuff they've prepared. If I was younger and still had my health they wouldn't dare treat me like this. I'd have my own book. But there you go just because I smell funny and can't make it to the toilet in time. PUNKS.

44

STAN'S RIGHT TO
HAVE BABIES

A Roman amphitheatre. The REVOLUTIONARIES – REG, FRANCIS, STAN *and* JUDITH, *are seated in the stands. They speak conspiratorially.*

JUDITH: . . . Any Anti-Imperialist group like ours must *reflect* such a divergence of interests within its power-base.

REG: Agreed.

General nodding.

Francis?

FRANCIS: I think Judith's point of view is valid here, Reg, provided the Movement never forgets that it is the inalienable right of every man . . .

STAN: Or woman.

FRANCIS: Or woman . . . to rid himself . . .

STAN: Or herself.

REG: Or herself. Agreed. Thank you, brother.

STAN: Or sister.

FRANCIS: Thank you, brother. Or sister. Where was I?

REG: I thought you'd finished.

FRANCIS: Oh did I? Right.

REG: Furthermore, it is the birthright of every man . . .

STAN: Or woman.

REG: Why don't you shut up about women, Stan, you're putting us off.

STAN: Women have a perfect right to play a part in our movement, Reg.

FRANCIS: Why are you always on about women, Stan?

STAN: . . . I want to be one.

REG: . . . What?

STAN: I want to be a woman. From now on I want you all to call me Loretta.

REG: What!?

STAN: It's my right as a man.

JUDITH: Why do you want to be Loretta, Stan?

STAN: I want to have babies.

REG: You want to have babies????!!!

STAN: It's every man's right to have babies if he wants them.

REG: But you can't have babies.

STAN: Don't you oppress me.

REG: I'm not oppressing you. Stan – you haven't got a womb. Where's the foetus going to gestate? You going to keep it in a box?

STAN *starts crying.*

JUDITH: Here! I've got an idea. Suppose you agree that he can't actually have babies, not having a womb, which is nobody's fault, not even the Romans', but that he can have the *right* to have babies.

FRANCIS: Good idea, Judith. We shall fight the oppressors for your right to have babies, brother. Sister, sorry.

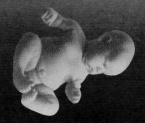

REG: What's the point?

FRANCIS: What?

REG: What's the point of fighting for his right to have babies, when he can't have babies?

FRANCIS: It is symbolic of our struggle against oppression.

REG: It's symbolic of his struggle against reality.

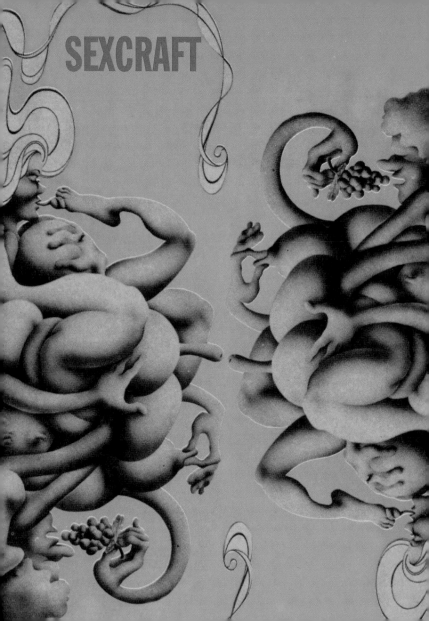

SEXCRAFT

THE VIBRA-PHONE:

GPO permission needed Contact your friends at intimate moments. Let them hear *how* you miss them. Dial TIM, or the weather forecast. Dial LONDON TOURIST INFORMATION, or The Latest Test Score without interrupting your private life.

VIBRADIO:

Current Radio Licence required in the British Isles. *Why Miss Your Favourites?* Listen to the Archers as never before. Contribute to 'Any Answers' without leaving the comfort of your own bed (or somebody else's).
VHF:
Car Model Also Available, Plugs in the Mains. Just watch it go. Lasts a whole weekend without any messy battery changes.

THE 'THOMPSON' WALLET SUPPORTER:

For the maturer man who finds his freedom of movement restricted by the size of his wallet. The 'THOMPSON' Wallet Supporter gives uplift in 3 vital areas: (a) credit cards (b) huge wads of fivers and (c) freds. With the 'THOMPSON' Wallet Supporter even the most successful businessman can jump and roll around unfettered.

THE 'ALADDIN':

No more tiresome ejaculations! The 'ALADDIN' produces a realistic squeal, as of a pig being trodden on, at the crucial moment, thereby distracting your partner's attention, and providing YOU with an alibi.

THE 'WIDGERY' BLACKMAIL NOTE:

A really safe document. (Guaranteed untraceable – contains no ex-works no. or address) Simply fill in the amount required, the name of the blackmailee, the place to leave the money, and some rough indication of the sexual practice to be revealed, in the spaces provided on the note, and 'hey-presto!' you're rich overnight!

THE 'GROSVENOR' ARM CHAIR:

A real post-coital 'must' for all active people. After a good bang, sit down and relax in the 'Grosvenor' Range of Furniture. 'A really comfortable armchair' *The Sun* ('Grosvenor' Post-Coital Products, Brighton)

SHEATHS etc.

THE OMAR SHEATH:
Uncircumcised
rubberware

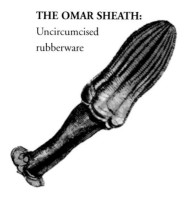

THE WHOOPEE-SHEATH:
Makes a rude noise when sat on.
Startle your friends.

THE 'WHAT'S THAT SONNY?':
For the smaller man.

THE PROTECTORS:
Thursdays. Television Series. ATV

THE PATRIOT'S PROTECTOR:
Available in red, white and blue.
Also:
Stars and Stripes
Union Jack
Tricolour
Hammer and Sickle
Maple Leaf

JOINT:
This one's for passing around.

THE BOSTON STARTLER:
Available for the larger gentleman.
In several colours: black, brown and
Australian.

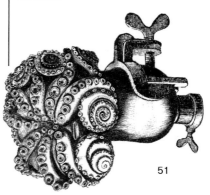

WHY ACCOUNTANCY
IS NOT BORING

Why accountancy is not boring by Mr A. Putey

First let me say how very pleased I was to be asked on the 14th inst. to write an article on why accountancy is not boring. I feel very very strongly that there are many people who may think that accountancy *is* boring, but they would be wrong, for it is not at all boring, as I hope to show you in this article, which is, as I intimated earlier, a pleasure to write.

I think I can do little worse than begin this article by describing why accountancy is *not* boring as far as *I* am concerned, and then, perhaps, go on to a more general discussion of why accountancy as a whole is not boring. As soon as I awake in the morning it is not boring. I get up at 7.16, and my wife Irene, an ex-schoolteacher, gets up shortly afterwards at 7.22. Breakfast is far from boring, and soon I am ready to leave the house. Irene, a keen Rotarian, hands me my briefcase and rolled umbrella at 7.53, and I leave the house seconds later. It is a short walk to Sutton station, but by no means a boring one. There is so much to see, including Mr Edgeworth, who also works at Robinson Partners. Mr Edgeworth is an extremely interesting man, and was in Uxbridge during the war. I think that many of the people to whom accountancy appears boring think that all accountants are the same. Nothing could be further from the truth. Some accountants are chartered, but very many others are certified. I am a certified accountant, as indeed is Mr Edgeworth, whom I told you about earlier. However, in the next office to mine is a Mr Manners, who is a chartered accountant, and, incidentally, a keen Rotarian. So far, as you can see, accountancy is not boring. During the morning there are a hundred and one things to do. A secretary may pop in with details of an urgent audit. This happened in 1967 and again last year. On the other hand, the phone may ring, or there may be details of a new superannuation scheme to mull over. The time flies by in this not at all boring way, and it is soon 10.00, when there is only 1 hour to go before Mrs Jackson brings round the tea urn. At 11.05, having drunk an interesting cup of tea, I put my cup on the tray and then . . .

(18 *pages deleted here* – Ed.) . . . and once the light is turned out by Irene, a very keen Rotarian, I am left to think about how extremely un-boring my day has been, being an accountant. Finally may I say how extremely grateful I am to your book for so generously allowing me so much space. (*Sorry, Putey!* – Ed.)

IN THE TOWER

A young, quite embarrassingly unattractive PRINCE *is gazing out of a castle window. His* FATHER *stands beside him. He is also looking out.*

FATHER: One day lad, all this will be yours . . .

PRINCE: What – the curtains?

FATHER: No! Not the curtains, lad . . . all that . . . *(he indicates the vista from the window)* all that you can see, stretched out over the hills and valleys . . . as far as the eye can see and beyond . . . that'll be your kingdom, lad.

PRINCE: But, Mother . . .

FATHER: Father, lad.

PRINCE: But, Father, I don't want any of that, I'd rather . . .

FATHER: Rather what?

PRINCE: I'd rather . . . just . . . sing . . .

Music starts.

FATHER: You're not going into a song while I'm here!

Music stops.

Listen, lad, in twenty minutes you're going to be married to a girl whose father owns the biggest tracts of open land in Britain . . .

PRINCE: I don't want land.

FATHER: Listen, Alice . . .

PRINCE: Herbert.

FATHER: Herbert . . . You're marrying Princess Lucky, so you'd better get used to the idea! Guards!

TWO GUARDS *enter and stand to attention on either side of the door. One of them has hiccoughs.*

FATHER: Make sure the Prince doesn't leave this room until I come and get him.

FIRST GUARD: Not . . . to leave the room . . . even if you come and get him.

FATHER: No. *Until* I come and get him.

SECOND GUARD: Hic.

FIRST GUARD: Until you come and get him, we're not to enter the room.

FATHER: No . . . You stay in the room and make sure he doesn't leave.

FIRST GUARD: . . . and you'll come and get him.

SECOND GUARD: Hic.

FATHER: That's right.

FIRST GUARD: We don't need to do anything apart from just stop him entering the room.

FATHER: Leaving the room.

FIRST GUARD: Leaving the room . . .yes.

FATHER: Got it?

SECOND GUARD: Hic.

FIRST GUARD: Er . . . if . . . we . . . er . . .

FATHER: Yes?

FIRST GUARD: If we . . . er . . . *(trying to remember what he was going to say)*

FATHER: Look, it's simple. Just stay here and make sure he doesn't leave the room.

SECOND GUARD: Hic.

FATHER: Right?

FIRST GUARD: Oh, I remember . . . can he . . . er . . . can he leave the room *with* us?

FATHER *(carefully)*: No . . . keep him in here . . . and make sure he doesn't . . .

FIRST GUARD: Oh, yes! We'll keep him in here, obviously. But if he *had* to leave . . . and we were with him.

FATHER: No . . . just keep him in here.

FIRST GUARD: Until you, or anyone else . . .

FATHER: No. Not anyone else – just me.

FIRST GUARD: Just you . . .

SECOND GUARD: Hic.

FIRST GUARD: Get back.

FATHER: Right.

FIRST GUARD: Okay. Fine. We'll remain here until you get back.

FATHER: And make sure he doesn't leave.

FIRST GUARD: What?

FATHER: Make sure he doesn't leave.

FIRST GUARD: The Prince . . .?

FATHER: Yes . . . make sure . . .

FIRST GUARD: Oh yes, of course! I thought you meant *him*!

(He points to the other GUARD *and laughs to himself.)* . . . you know, it seemed a bit daft me having to guard him when he's a guard . . .

FATHER: Is that clear?

SECOND GUARD: Hic.

FIRST GUARD: Oh, yes. That's quite clear. No problem.

FATHER *pulls open the door and makes to leave the room. The* GUARDS *follow.*

FATHER *(to the* GUARDS*)*: Where are you going?

FIRST GUARD: We're coming with you.

FATHER: No, I want you to stay here and make sure he doesn't leave the room until I get back.

FIRST GUARD: Oh, I see, right.

They take up positions on either side of the door.

PRINCE: But, Father.

FATHER: Shut your noise, you, and get that suit on!

He points to a wedding suit on a chair. FATHER *throws one last look at the* PRINCE *and turns, goes out and slams the door.*

The PRINCE *slumps on to a window seat, looking forlornly out of the window. . . .*

Music starts . . .

The door flies open, the music cuts off and FATHER *pokes his head in.*

FATHER: And NO SINGING!

SECOND GUARD: Hic.

FATHER *(as he goes out)*: Go and have a drink of water.

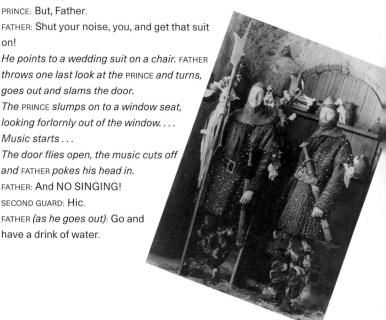

58

I'm so worried about what's happening today
In the Middle East, you know
And I'm so worried about the baggage retrieval
System they've got at Heathrow.

I'm so worried about the fashions today
I don't think they're good for your feet
And I'm so worried about the shows on TV
That sometimes they want to repeat.

 I'm so worried about what's happening today, you know
And I'm worried about the baggage retrieval
System they've got at Heathrow . . .

I'm so worried about modern technology
I'm so worried about all the things that they dump in the sea
I'm so worried about it, worried about it,
Worried, worried, worried . . .

I'm so worried about everything that can go wrong
I'm so worried about whether people like this song
I'm so worried about this very next verse
It isn't the best that I've got
And I'm so worried about whether I should go on
Or whether I shouldn't just stop.

PUBLISHER'S WARNING

Page 59 is missing, believed to be
held captive by a breakaway group
of terrorists loyal to page 29. They
have threatened to cut off a piece of
the page and send it back to the
publishers every day until their
demands are met.

I'm worried about whether I ought to have stopped
And I'm worried because it's the sort of thing I ought to know
And I'm so worried about the baggage retrieval
System they've got at Heathrow.

I'm so worried about whether I should have stopped then
I'm so worried that I'm driving everyone round the bend
I'm worried about the baggage retrieval
System they've got at Heathrow.

INDEX

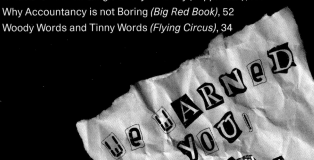

WE WARNED YOU!

hing a limp thoroughl
nd placing the tongue in b
thereby creating £10,000,0
ich and prosperous with me

59

A PREFACE BY ERIC IDLE FOR PEOPLE WHO HAVE MISTAKENLY OPENED THIS BOOK UPSIDE DOWN AND BACK TO FRONT

I cannot believe these people are seriously trying to rip you off once again by banging out selected passages from old Python books. I mean have they no shame? It's not like this stuff was any good the first time around, but to reprint it and shovel it out once more, well whatever is next? Python in Urdu? Ancient Flying Circus skits in Braille? The Best of the Finest Reprinted Sketches hand tinted and printed backwards for your reading pleasure? Maybe they'll broaden the concept – Michael Palin's Best Bits of the Bible or John Cleese's Highlights from Shakespeare, or Terry Jones' favourite fictional shags.

This one is apparently edited by someone called Terry Gilliam. I don't remember him, but one of my scantily-clad, tiny, but perfectly formed, Philippino assistants has just come off the Internet with the interesting information that he is apparently an unemployed film director and once did the disgusting drawings for the Python shows. Oh yes now I remember him, he had long hair and rather a cute little ass . . . I never knew he could read. And now he's *editing*? Still, it's your money, or *was* until you plonked it down for this piece of unadulterated garbage. So don't come running to me, moaning and grumbling about how you've been ripped off because I don't stand to gain one single penny . . . what? Really? *How much?* Wow. Okay. This is one of the finest books in the world. Lovingly hand edited by the genius of Terry Gilliam this wonderful piece of work will bring you hours and hours of sheer unadulterated pleasure. I can thoroughly recommend it to everybody in the entire world.

E.I. February 2000